Not Forgotten:
A Tribute to Memories and Caring

Written and Illustrated by Honey Miller

Copyright 2018 Honey Miller

ISBN-13: 978-0-9994518-2-3

DEDICATION

This book is dedicated to the many individuals who have cared for someone living with a dementia diagnosis.

So day by day, we'll give our best to those who need His love.

and each day we will remember the Lord is on our side.

Thank you for the light of memories.
Thank you for the light of love.
Thank you for the light of caring.

In 2008 my life was forever changed as I accepted a position as an activity director in a memory care assisted living facility. In the first few weeks, I literally cried on my way home most every day. I found myself staying beyond my regular hours in hopes that maybe I could help bring an extra smile or two at the end of the day. In November of that year, I experienced my first National Alzheimer's Awareness Month. Since I was regularly singing and playing guitar for the residents, I was asked to select and provide the music for a candle lighting ceremony. I searched and searched for a song but I just could not find the right one that expressed the deep emotion and life changing events I had experienced as a dementia caregiver.

So I wrote my own.

This book is that song. It is the exact song I wrote for that event in the fall of 2008. It is a threefold tribute beginning with that person who was diagnosed with Alzheimer's or some other form of dementia, and has passed from us. It also is a tribute to family members as they care for or remember a loved one who relied on them at life's end. And finally it is a tribute to the professionals who dedicate themselves day in and day out, ensuring that those diagnosed with cognitive decline have the best quality of life possible. With God all things are possible. He is our help in times of trouble. He is our light in the darkness.

Honey Miller

www.ingramcontent.com/pod-product-compliance
Lightning Source LLC
Chambersburg PA
CBHW041543040426
42446CB00002B/211